Lent & Easter

Catholic Customs and Traditions

by
Joanna Bogle

*All booklets are published thanks to the
generous support of the members of the
Catholic Truth Society*

CATHOLIC TRUTH SOCIETY
PUBLISHERS TO THE HOLY SEE

Contents

A rich heritage

Springtime brings Lent and Easter. Every year, as the new growth arrives on the trees, and plants begin to shoot up in the earth, the Church celebrates the great events of Christ's passion, death and Resurrection.

The heart of Christianity

These events concern the drama of our salvation. "God, infinitely perfect and blessed in himself, in a plan of sheer goodness, freely created man to make him share in his own blessed life. In the fullness of time, God the Father sent his Son as the Redeemer and Saviour of mankind, fallen into sin, thus calling all into his Church and, through the work of the Holy Spirit, making them adopted children and heirs of his eternal happiness."[1]

The great events of Christ's passion, death and resurrection are the fulfilment of God's plan. Each year, the Church calls us to a fresh commemoration and understanding of these things. It is not just a sort of annual remembrance, but something far deeper: Christ died for our sins and rose again, and this "Easter Mystery" is at the heart of our faith.

---

[1] *Compendium of the Catechism of the Catholic Church.*

When Christ established his Church, he told his apostles to take the message to everyone. The Church spread through the routes of the Roman Empire, reaching Britain, for example, at quite an early date - certainly at some time within the first century and a half after Christ's resurrection. Ever since that time, the Mass has been celebrated and the glorious mysteries of the Faith taught to each new generation.

The date of Easter is linked to that of the Jewish Passover. Easter Sunday is always the first Sunday after the first full moon of the year, or after the Spring Equinox. The Spring Equinox - when there are equal hours of day and of night - is 21st March. Thus Easter can fall at any time between 22nd March and 25th April.

Lost symbols and signs

Over the centuries, many traditions and customs have become associated with Lent and Easter, surrounding the Church's own rich liturgy for the season. Today, however, Christians will often find themselves living side by side with people for whom Lent and Easter may mean very little. Easter eggs will often be on sale in the shops from late January onwards, and there are also specially-boxed chocolates, and cards showing rabbits and daffodils. The Easter weekend is a holiday for everyone. But what is it all about? It is so often the case that a good number of Catholics can remain confused and muddled among all this activity - and they will probably learn very little about the true meaning of Lent and Easter from the television or the consumer culture that surrounding them.

Which customs and traditions have real meaning, and which are merely recent commercially-backed innovations? How can we grasp the real meaning of Lent and Easter, without seeming to be priggish and over-pious? Is it true that some of the traditions - like Pancake Day and rolling Easter eggs downhill - have Christian origins? How can we find out more?

Rediscovering a rich heritage

Many - in fact most - of the customs and traditions associated with Easter have strong Christian roots. It is worth taking time to find out more, to grasp the essential message of this season and to discover how earlier traditions and customs fit into the picture, and how we can all use this precious time to understand better the great truths of the Christian Faith, and help to spread its message to everyone.

Discovering the origins of some of our Lenten and Easter customs can enrich our faith, and learning more about them can be fascinating - as well as providing a whole range of ways in which to celebrate this holy season in our homes, parishes, and schools.

Shrovetide

The 'joyful season' of Lent is the period of forty days during which Christians prepare for their great Feast of Feasts: Easter. The old name for the few days just before Lent is "Shrovetide". This refers to people going to confession and being "shriven" of their sins. The verb "to shrive" comes from the same root as "scribe" and "scrape", and the German word "schreib" which means to write. In the days of quill pens, scraping and inscribing were linked. Vellum (fine parchment made from animal skin) had to be scraped before it was possible to write on it, and writing itself then involved scraping a sharp quill pen, dipped in ink, across the page. When we are cleansed of our sins in confession, we are as it were "scraped" clean.

In Evelyn Waugh's *Sword of Honour* trilogy, one of the characters says he will be going to confession as he needs "a scrape" before going to Holy Communion. In Shakespeare's *Hamlet*, the Prince's chief concern about his father is that he died without time to be "shriven" of his sins.

Shrove Tuesday

Lent begins on Ash Wednesday, and the day before is known as "Shrove Tuesday". On that day, in medieval times, a bell would be rung at church to announce that the priest was hearing confessions. It was the "shriving bell". Today, the arrival of Shrovetide and Lent is still a personal call to conversion, a time when we are reminded of the need to repent and confess our sins.

Pancake Day

Shrove Tuesday is often called Pancake Day. It is a long-established custom that we eat pancakes on this day - traditionally with lemon juice and brown sugar, but also perhaps with hot chocolate sauce and ice-cream, or any other delicious combination. Why pancakes? It is because Lent is a season of fasting. So the tradition is that we finish up all the dairy products we have - specifically eggs and milk and cream - in a great meal before Lent when the call to fasting begins. Incidentally, that is partly how the tradition of Easter eggs began: people didn't eat eggs during Lent, so they were saved up, and became a big part of the Easter celebrations.

In her autobiographical book *The Sound of Music* - which of course gave rise to a popular musical and film - Maria von Trapp described how Lent was observed in Austria, and other Catholic parts of Europe, by devout people in the early days of the 20th century. In keeping with age-old traditions, people gave up meat, eggs, and all dairy foods such as cheese and milk.

Mardi gras carnival

The French name for Shrovetide is *Mardi gras* - "Fat Tuesday", again reflecting the idea of people enjoying good food before the fasting began on Ash Wednesday. The other name for Shrovetide is carnival, from the Latin *carni*, meaning meat, and *vale*, meaning goodbye. It's goodbye to meat for the whole of Lent! Each spring there are famous carnivals in various parts of Europe and Latin America, but they are no longer linked with Lent. However, some of the imagery of carnival reminds us of the original Lenten connection. Think of a traditional carnival pierrot clown - he usually has a tear painted on his cheek, signifying the notion of a party and celebration which will nevertheless have a solemn ending - the Mardi gras carnival which ends at midnight as Ash Wednesday starts and the mood suddenly changes. And think of the song *"The carnival is over..."* The tradition of carnival always somehow includes the notion that it ends with a time of sorrow - the feasting and merriment end with Lent.

Collop Monday

Eating pancakes and having a Mardi gras party is a good way to bring people together before Lent begins. It is traditional to toss each pancake three times (in honour of the Trinity). There can be lots of different pancake fillings - savoury as well as sweet - and people can enjoy trying their hand at frying the pancakes. For the savoury pancakes, ham and mushrooms make a good filling. Long ago, when meat had to be preserved through the winter by salting it, the last pieces of ham that were eaten up as spring arrived, were known as "collops" and the day before Shrove Tuesday was "Collop Monday".

In the right spirit

But the party only really makes sense if we are going to honour the true purpose of Lent itself. Today it can be unrealistic for some people to give up all meat and dairy products. But the Church still calls us to penance during Lent. It is not optional. We are invited to take seriously the call to repent, fast and make sacrifices. And this is not just a personal thing - it is something we do together, with the whole community of the Church around the world. As our Mardi gras celebrations end, there is a solemn note. No more feasting after midnight: Lent has started.

Season of Lent

"As we approach the season of Lent and the days leading to the Easter festival which focuses attention on the mysteries of our redemption, the need for religious preparation is proclaimed... These forty days which have been instituted by the Apostles should be given over to fasting. This means not just reducing food which benefits soul and body, but the elimination of unworthy habits. To these we should add almsgiving which, under the name of mercy, covers a multitude of praiseworthy deeds of charity. So all the faithful, though unequal in worldly possessions, are equal; in the inspiration of their spiritual lives and can achieve an equal standing in loving all their brothers and sisters in the human race... if we show love to those in any kind of distress then we are blessed with the virtue of charity and are at peace." (*Pope Leo the Great* d. 461)

The forty days

In the Old Testament, Moses led the people of Israel for forty years through the desert. In the New Testament, Christ spent forty days in the desert in prayer before the start of his public ministry. Numbers are very important in the Scriptures, and the Church's times and seasons reflect this. Lent is forty days long, covering a period of six weeks. You can count up the days on a calendar, starting from Ash Wednesday and leaving out the six Sundays, which brings you to Holy Saturday, the day before Easter Sunday. Each Sunday is a little Easter, a Day of Lord, and cannot be counted as an ordinary part of Lent. Some parishes provide special "Lenten charts" for children: these have boxes to colour in, one for each day, each box suggesting some special activity or small penance for that day: "Today I will do a secret good turn to someone" "Today I will not complain about *anything*" "No television today". Such a chart could also be made at home or at school.

During Lent we will not use the word "Alleluia" in our prayers at Mass, and we will not be singing the *Gloria*. Both of these are exclamations of joy and therefore not suitable for this season of penance.

'Lent'

The English word "Lent" is of Saxon origin - like the word "shrove" above - and refers to the fact that the days are starting to *lengthen* at this time of year. In Italian, the word is *Quaresima*, referring to the forty days. In German, it is *Fastenzeit*, fasting-time.

Why fast in Lent?

Fasting is a central part of Lent. We are meant to eat less and deny ourselves luxuries. We are meant to renounce even good things - cream, meat, sweets - because we are seeking to become closer to God. Even people who are not Catholics are aware of the tradition of "giving up" something during this season. But we need to understand what fasting and penance are all about:

"In our own day, fasting seems to have lost something of its spiritual meaning, and has taken on, in a culture characterised by the search for material well-being, a therapeutic value for the care of one's body. Fasting certainly brings benefits to physical well-being, but for believers, it is, in the first place, a "therapy" to heal all that prevents them from conformity to the will of God." (*Pope Benedict XVI*, 2009)

Jesus himself fasted, and showed us that this is a way to overcome evil and also to draw very close to God. It is an aid to prayer and a rebuke to Satan.

"The Gospels speak of a time of solitude for Jesus in the desert immediately after his baptism by John. Driven by the Spirit into the desert, Jesus remains there for forty days without eating; he lives among wild beasts, and angels minister to him. At the end of this time Satan tempts him three times, seeking to compromise his filial attitude towards God. Jesus rebuffs these attacks, which recapitulate the temptations of Adam in Paradise and of the Israelites in the desert, and the devil leaves him 'until an opportune time.'"

Penance and conversion

The major theme and purpose of Lent is to offer Christians a time for penance and conversion, in preparation for the Easter feast itself and the fifty days of Eastertide that follow. Catholics are urged to confess their sins during Lent, and receive absolution. This is linked to the obligation that we must receive Holy Communion at least once a year, at Easter or thereabouts. The old expression for this is "Easter duties".[2]

All Catholic churches have extra opportunities for confession during Lent. Some parishes arrange special evenings when a number of priests come to the church to hear confessions, with prayers and a short sermon beforehand to help people prepare.

Catholic schools and organisations often arrange similar Penitential Services during Lent. Major centres of pilgrimage, big city parishes, and cathedrals, will have special arrangements for confession during this season too.

"The confession (or disclosure) of sins, even from a simply human point of view, frees us and facilitates our reconciliation with others. Through such an admission man looks squarely at the sins of which he is guilty, takes

---

[2] The five precepts of the Church include: "2. You shall confess your sins at least once a year" and "3. You shall receive the Sacrament of the Eucharist at least during the Easter season." See *Compendium of the Catholic Church*, "Formulas of Catholic Doctrine".

responsibility for them, and thereby opens himself again to God and to the communion of the Church in order to make a new future possible."[3]

Spring cleaning

Springtime has long been associated with "spring cleaning", in both the Christian and Jewish traditions, when we turn out our houses, throw away rubbish, and think about cleaning and redecorating. Lent is an opportunity for some "spiritual spring cleaning"!

> "God, the Father of mercies
> Through the death and resurrection of his Son
> Has reconciled the world to himself
> And sent the Holy Spirit among us
> For the forgiveness of sins;
> Through the ministry of the Church
> May God grant you pardon and peace,
> And I absolve you from your sins
> In the name of the Father and of the Son
> And of the Holy Spirit."[4]

---

[3] *Catechism of the Catholic Church* 1455

[4] Formula of absolution

Ash Wednesday

Ashes are an ancient symbol of sorrow and mourning. Ashes are all that is left when something is burned. Ashes take us to the very end of things, to death and finality. Using Biblical language, we still sometimes speak of some one "wearing sackcloth and ashes" when they are publicly repenting of something.

"Blow the trumpet in Zion;
　　sound the alarm on my holy mountain!
Let all the inhabitants of the land tremble,
　　for the day of the Lord is coming, it is near—
a day of darkness and gloom,
　　a day of clouds and thick darkness!
Like blackness spread upon the mountains
　　a great and powerful army comes;
their like has never been from of old,
　　nor will be again after them in ages to come.

Yet even now, says the Lord,
　　return to me with all your heart,
with fasting, with weeping, and with mourning;
　　rend your hearts and not your clothing.
Return to the Lord, your God,
　　for he is gracious and merciful,

slow to anger, and abounding in steadfast love,
and relents from punishing.
Who knows whether he will not turn and relent,
and leave a blessing behind him,
a grain-offering and a drink-offering
for the Lord, your God?"[5]

A day of fasting

Ash Wednesday is the first day of Lent. The Church decrees that it is a day of fasting and abstinence. This means that all adult Catholics - those aged 14 to 65 - must fast, and abstain from all meat and meat products. That is not very difficult to do: more precisely the Church explains that such fasting means one main cooked meal, and two light snacks. It is not a difficult rule to obey. In fact, more importantly, we should obey its spirit, and make sure we really are eating much less than we would normally do. Traditional dishes for the main meal on Ash Wednesday are fish pie or vegetable casserole. The sick and infirm do not have to fast or abstain.

The ashes

On Ash Wednesday, often at Mass, the priest distributes ashes on our foreheads, saying "Remember man, that you

---

[5] *Joel* 2:1-2, used in the liturgy for Ash Wednesday

are dust and to dust you shall return" or "Repent, and believe in the Gospel".

The ashes are made from the palms from the previous year's Palm Sunday, and are blessed at the beginning of Mass or at the main Mass of the day.

The priest and/or deacon takes a dish of the ashes and as we go forward one by one, he marks our foreheads with ash, making the sign of the Cross. This happens in every Catholic church around the world. The Pope receives the ashes in this way too, - you can even watch the ceremony on the internet.

Called to prayer, fasting and almsgiving

During Lent the Church calls us to penance, prayer, and almsgiving. "Alms" is the old-fashioned word for giving funds for charity, helping the poor and the sick. Until quite recently, the social worker attached to a hospital was still known as an "almoner".

During Lent, we are each meant to fast and to practice some form of penance: giving up sweets or snacks or alcohol, or perhaps some small luxury such as a favourite magazine or regular stops at a coffee-shop - and the money saved should be given to charity as alms. Even if our chosen penances do not involve saving and giving money, and we might also decide to renounce or 'give up' things we like; such as watching television, or spending time surfing the internet, almsgiving remains a central part of Lent.

"At the same time, fasting is an aid to open our eyes to the situation in which so many of our brothers and sisters live. In his *First Letter*, St John admonishes: "If anyone has the world's goods, and sees his brother in need, yet shuts up his bowels of compassion from him - how does the love of God abide in him?"(3,17). Voluntary fasting enables us to grow in the spirit of the Good Samaritan, who bends low and goes to the help of his suffering brother (cf. Encyclical *Deus Caritas Est* 15). By freely embracing an act of self-denial for the sake of another, we make a statement that our brother or sister in need is not a stranger. It is precisely to keep alive this welcoming and attentive attitude towards our brothers and sisters, that I encourage the parishes and every other community to intensify in Lent the custom of private and communal fasts, joined to the reading of the Word of God, prayer and almsgiving. From the beginning, this has been the hallmark of the Christian community, in which special collections were taken up (cf. 2 *Co* 8-9; *Rm* 15, 25-27), the faithful being invited to give to the poor what had been set aside from their fast (*Didascalia Ap.*, V, 20,18). This practice needs to be rediscovered and encouraged again in our day, especially during the liturgical season of Lent." (*Pope Benedict XVI* 2009)

Obviously, all this is linked to prayer. Many people will make an extra effort to go to daily Mass during Lent, or to drop into church to pray, or to say the Rosary regularly, or to join in the Church's formal Office of Morning and Evening Prayer, at home or with others.

In secret

The penance we do in Lent is not something we should ever boast about, or even allow to be known. That's part of the tradition, and what Jesus tells us in the Gospel. The aim is not to draw attention to ourselves or to what we are doing, and to carry on as normal - any public parade of piety, any ostentatious marching to early Mass, missal in hand, or the waving away of chocolates when proffered, is not in the spirit of the thing at all!

"When you fast, do not put on a gloomy look as the hypocrites do; they pull long faces to let men know they are fasting. I tell you solemnly, they have their reward. But when you fast, put oil on your head and wash your face, so that no one will know you are fasting except your Father in heaven who sees all that is done in secret; and your Father who sees all that is done in secret will reward you." (*Mt* 6:16-18)

Communal activities

There is also a communal side to Lent, especially so because we are members of the worldwide Church. Family prayers said together in the evening, or a family rosary said in the car, or friends meeting at church on a Friday evening to pray the Stations of the Cross can become traditions.

Schools and Catholic groups will often organise special Lenten events - lunchtime prayers, talks on Lenten themes, boxes for Lenten alms that are then sent to a charity.

During Lent, those who are entering the Church - adult converts who are preparing for baptism, or who are being received into full communion with the Catholic Church, after being brought up in a non-Catholic denomination - will be welcomed into the final stages of their journey. They will be baptised at Easter. Of course it is possible to be baptised and to become a Catholic at any time of the year, but many people choose to join a group that makes this journey together, in this special season.

Pilgrimage and retreat

Many Catholic parishes organise a Day of Recollection or even a full weekend retreat during Lent. Spending time at a place of retreat run by a religious community can re-charge spiritual batteries. Lent is also a time when some people go on pilgrimage - perhaps a simple walk with friends to a shrine or special church, praying together on the way and making the Stations of the Cross. Most parishes will stock booklets during Lent with ideas for these and similar activities.

"Penance can be expressed in many and various ways but above all in fasting, prayer, and almsgiving. These and many other forms of penance can be practised in the daily life of a Christian, particularly during the time of Lent and on the penitential day of Friday."[6]

Friendship with God

"We might wonder what value and meaning there is for us Christians in depriving ourselves of something that in itself is good and useful for our bodily sustenance. The Sacred Scriptures and the entire Christian tradition teach that fasting is a great help to avoid sin and all that leads to it. For this reason, the history of salvation is replete with occasions that invite fasting. In the very first pages of Sacred Scripture, the Lord commands man to abstain from partaking of the prohibited fruit: "You may freely eat of every tree of the garden; but of the tree of the knowledge of good and evil you shall not eat, for in the day that you eat of it you shall die" (*Gn* 2, 16-17). Commenting on the divine injunction, St Basil observes that "fasting was ordained in Paradise," and "the first commandment in this sense was delivered to Adam." He thus concludes: " 'You shall not eat' is a law of fasting and abstinence" (cf. *Sermo de jejunio: PG* 31, 163, 98). Since all of us are weighed down by sin and its consequences, fasting is proposed to us as an instrument to restore friendship with God." (*Pope Benedict XVI*, 2009)

---

[6] *Compendium of the Catechism of the Catholic Church*, 301

Yet a great many others will not be aware of Lent or observing it at all. As we know, the shops will be full of Easter bunnies, Easter eggs and other chocolate items. There will be talk of special Easter holiday weekend bargains at resorts and hotels. There will be nothing in the shops to remind us that this festivity is preceded by a season of penance and fasting.

However, the Church comes to our help in celebrating the seasons, and Lent is no exception. In union with Christians around the world and down the centuries, we can benefit greatly from a period of inner conversion and obedience to God's call.

"He who does not keep the fast in Lent is guilty of prevarication". (*St Ambrose* 340-397)

The Stations of the Cross

An important devotion in Lent is the Stations of the Cross. This is an ancient way of following Christ on his path to Calvary. Long ago, pilgrims to the Holy Land would walk the route that Christ himself took as he carried his Cross to the hill where he died. They took the tradition home with them, and the Church established the fourteen "stations", visual images to be contemplated, as a devotion for people who could not travel to the Holy Land itself.

Today, Catholic churches have the fourteen Stations depicted around the walls, and "praying the stations" brings people together, most often on a Friday, during Lent. The Stations can also be prayed individually and silently, or by two or three friends joining together, or even in bigger groups. There are small booklets with prayers and meditations for each Station.

In some places, there are outdoor Stations of the Cross, where you can walk through woods or around a garden as you follow Christ's path to Calvary. It is also possible simply to follow the stations prayerfully in a book while on a train journey or sitting at home.

Following Christ to Calvary in this way is a very powerful way of meditating on what he did for us, and it draws us close to him. Actually walking around a church, stopping at each Station and reading the appropriate prayers and meditation, gives us a sense of unity with Christ as he walked the painful route to Calvary. Christ's trial before Pilate, his cruel journey carrying the heavy cross, his meeting with his mother and with the women of Jerusalem, all become events that are not remote from us. It is traditional to remain in silent prayer for an extra period when we reach the twelfth station, Christ's actual death on the Cross.

The Stations of the Cross

1. Jesus is condemned to death.
2. Jesus is given his cross
3. Jesus falls the first time
4. Jesus meets his mother
5. Simon of Cyrene helps Jesus to carry the cross
6. Veronica wipes the face of Jesus
7. Jesus falls the second time
8. Jesus meets the women of Jerusalem
9. Jesus falls the third time
10. Jesus is stripped of his garments
11. The Crucifixion: Jesus is nailed to the cross
12. Jesus dies on the cross
13. Jesus' body is taken down from the cross
14. Jesus is laid in the tomb.

Saints' days in Lent

Lent always includes the month of March, and that means that there can be a short pause from the Lenten fasting on some days if we wish - because March includes some important feast-days. On feast days fasting and penance gives way to a modest amount of rejoicing and celebration

Month of March

A saint's feast-day is usually celebrated on the anniversary of the day that he or she died. March feast-days include St David, the Patron Saint of Wales, on 1st March; St Patrick - Ireland's Patron - on 17th March; and St Joseph, foster-father of Christ, on 19th March. Each of these is associated with special traditions, foods, and symbols.

St David

St David's emblem is a leek or a daffodil - no one seems to know why. He is also associated with music, because of the great Welsh tradition of singing. He was a monk and founded a chain of monasteries across Wales, known for their austerity and holiness. St David's Day could be celebrated with a special supper - with leek-and-potato soup, or a leek pie (leeks in a cheese sauce with a puff-pastry topping)! This could be followed by "bara brith" (delicious Welsh fruitcake, served sliced with butter). A big bunch of daffodils as a centrepiece - and why not tell the story of St David as you enjoy the meal? David, or Dai or Dewi lived in the 6th century. He is said to have gone on pilgrimage to Jerusalem and was consecrated as Bishop there. He was certainly a Bishop, and established his see at the place now known as St David's in Pembrokeshire. He took part in a major Church council at Brefi in Cardigan, where he worked to reconcile different factions, so he is sometimes depicted with a dove. There are over fifty place-names in Wales associated with him, as well as places in Devon, Cornwall, and Brittany. Monks from Ireland studied under his direction and took his ideas and inspiration back to Ireland.

St Patrick

St Patrick's Day will be celebrated in style in Ireland, and in the places around the world where the Irish have settled, notably America. His symbol of the shamrock is linked to his teaching of the Trinity - he used the linked three leaves to teach about the Father, Son, and Holy Spirit. The traditional dish for St Patrick's Day is boiled bacon and cabbage. Some places brew special green beer in honour of the day! Patrick (born in about 380AD - no one knows for sure) was the son of a Romano-British chieftain, living on the west coast of Britain, probably in Wales. Carried off by raiders to Ireland, Patrick worked as a herdsman there, and when he was able to make his escape and reach home, he trained as a priest in order to return to Ireland to bring the Faith there. There are so many stories and legends about him - confronting the high king on Easter eve, kindling the Easter fire on the hill of Slane, silencing the druids, driving all the snakes out of Ireland. Consecrated as Bishop, he established his See at Armagh. The famous Croagh Patrick pilgrimage is based on the story of his 40-day retreat there. Irish music, a green tablecloth, a few shamrocks, and some storytelling - it's not difficult to arrange a St Patrick's supper for 17th March.

St Joseph

St Joseph is the Patron Saint of fathers, and honoured as such in many countries. He is also a Patron Saint for women seeking a good husband! An Italian tradition is to have a "St Joseph's Table" in the parish hall on this day, with a great array of donated sweets and goodies, preferably home-made. These are sold in aid of charity. Why not have such a table in your parish? Home-made toffee, fudge, and coconut-ice? Shortbread and flapjacks in nice ribboned boxes? People will need to buy goodies as Mothering Sunday gifts, or to store for Easter. Stacking up the table and making it look attractive is all part of the fun. You could decide to relax Lenten fasting for this one day, or be heroic and buy things to enjoy later.

The Annunciation

The feast of the Annunciation on 25th March also falls in Lent. This marks the day when Mary, as described in the Gospel of St Luke, was told by an angel that she was to be the mother of the Saviour. This is the day of the Incarnation, when Christ, the Son of God, arrived in his mother's womb.

The old English name for this day is "Lady Day" and for centuries it was marked as the first day of the New Year: in fact in a sense it still is, because our tax year runs from March to March each year. The Annunciation is exactly nine months before Christmas, signifying the time spent by Christ in the womb. An old tradition says that the first Good Friday was also on 25th March - Christ dying on the anniversary of the day on which he first arrived on earth.

Mothering Sunday: mid Lent

Lent can seem very long, and so there is a tradition that we take a mid-Lent break - a moment to stop and rest along the journey. The fourth Sunday in Lent is traditionally known as *Laetare* Sunday, from the Latin for "to rejoice". It is a day to take a break from the Lenten gloom. While the colour for the priest's vestments at Mass during Lent is purple - the colour of penance and sorrow - for this Sunday, the colour changes. The priest wears rose-coloured vestments, and these are very unusual - (not all parishes have them) as they are used only on this one Sunday in the year.

The day is sometimes known as "let-up Sunday" because we "let-up" on our Lenten penances. But it is far better known as Mothering Sunday - or, to give it the name by which it is mostly known nowadays, Mothers' Day.

Origins

Why is this particular Sunday set aside for honouring mothers? It is partly because of the ancient Romans. They had a festival of motherhood and fertility at this time of year. It was linked to the fact that the whole earth seemed to be fertile, with baby birds hatching from eggs and baby rabbits and lambs being born. The festival was known as *Matronalia*, and was celebrated by making cakes out of grains of cereal or pounded almonds. This grain was known as *similia* - the root which gives us the word *similar* (all the grains are alike) and from which the Italians get "semolina" and we get "simnel".

Simnel cake

A simnel cake is the traditional cake to bake for Mothering Sunday. It is a light fruit cake, with a layer of marzipan baked in the middle. Marzipan is, of course, made of ground almonds. The cake also has a layer of marzipan on top, and eleven small marzipan eggs round the edge - representing the Apostles, minus the traitor Judas. The cake is then placed under a light grill for a few moments, to give the marzipan eggs a brown speckled look, like real eggs.

The Church took over the pagan festivities, but gave them a whole new meaning. For Christians, motherhood is not essentially limited to fertility but is about the grace and dignity of being a Christian mother, teaching children the Faith and bringing them up to know, love, and serve God. The image for Christian mothers is that of Mary with the Christ child on her lap, giving to all mothers a status and dignity beyond anything imaginable in the ancient pagan world.

Flowers and eggs

Thus the mid-Lent break became a day for honouring mothers, and thus a holiday, a day to return to the family home and have a general family gathering. Over the centuries the day acquired various other customs - a bouquet of violets as a gift for Mother, a simnel cake - and a creamy egg custard as the traditional pudding at Sunday lunch on this day! Both simnel cake, and of course the custard, involve lots of eggs - again this is linked to the tradition of giving up eggs and dairy foods during Lent, and so having rather a lot to use up on this one day, when there is a break from the fasting.

Mother Church

Mothering Sunday was also a day for honouring Mother Church, and one tradition is that of visiting the cathedral, or Mother Church of the diocese, on this day. We need to understand the great reality of the Church as our Mother. We sometimes speak of the Church also as the "Bride of Christ" and St Paul tells us that the union between a man and his bride is like that of Christ and his Church. This is very important. Christ did indeed unite with his Bride, and this union is a fruitful one - all the baptised are the children of this marital union, and the Church is truly our Mother. There is a nuptial message which runs through the whole of our understanding of our redemption story. Pope John Paul II spoke of the "nuptial meaning" of the Eucharist.

An understanding of this will help us to grasp why marriage itself is so important, and why the Church recognises the lifelong union between a man and a woman as a sacrament and as something profoundly holy.

It will also help us to understand that God had a plan in making us male and female - it reveals a deeper mystery with a spiritual meaning.

Other influences

What gave a boost to Mothering Sunday, and effectively helped to re-invent it in the 20th century, was the arrival in Britain during World War II of large numbers of American servicemen. America has its own Mothers' Day in May, and these men brought this tradition with them. It had been formally invented in the 1900s by a lady named Anna Jarvis, who thought there should be a day when all mothers were honoured and chose her own mother's birthday as the date.

In wartime Britain, American airmen and soldiers came to know British families and on Mothering Sunday they produced gifts of chocolates and other small luxuries as a matter of course. The day took on a new significance and by the 1960s the idea of gifts and a treat for the mother of a family on that day was well established. From the 1980s and 90s onwards came the idea of larger gifts, or a meal out in a restaurant. It seems a pity if the day is just to become another opportunity for consumerism. In most families it really does mean much more, and most mothers and grandmothers cherish home-made cards and carefully-planned treats.

Prayers

It is usual to have special prayers for mothers said in church on this day, and in some parishes the priest blesses flowers which children then give to their mothers, or to all the women in the congregation as Mass ends. After Mass there can be simnel cake for everyone.

Palm Sunday

"All glory, laud, and honour to Christ, Redeemer, King,
to whom the lips of children made sweet hosannas ring!
The people of the Hebrews with palms adorned your way;
our praise and prayer and anthems we offer you this day.
All glory, laud, and honour to Christ, Redeemer, King!"
(*Hymn for Palm Sunday*)

Slowly the days of Lent pass, and the final week
approaches. It is Holy Week, when the whole Church
around the world commemorates the great events of
Christ's passion and death and resurrection. This is the
most important week of the Church's year.

Palms

The first day of Holy Week is Palm Sunday. On this day
we commemorate the triumphant entry of Christ into
Jerusalem. The people tore branches from the palm trees
to wave and to throw on the ground before him, to make a
carpet on which his donkey could ride. Today, we will
carry palm branches in procession as Mass begins. There
will be hymns such as "Ride on, ride on in majesty!"
Some parishes manage a procession down a local street,
for others it is around the car park or just across the land
separating the church from the parish hall.

"The next day a great crowd who had come to the feast heard that Jesus was coming to Jerusalem. So they took branches of palm trees and went out to meet him crying 'Hosanna! Blessed is he who comes in the name of the Lord, even the king of Israel!" (*Jn* 12:12-13)

Did you know that every donkey has a cross marked on its back? Check it out next time you see a donkey in a field or at a farm or zoo. It is there, clearly marked in the fur. Tradition says that this is because of the donkey that carried the Lord on that first Palm Sunday.

The palms we are given at Mass on Palm Sunday have been blessed and should be treated as holy objects. It is traditional to fold your Palm Sunday palm into a cross, which can then be tucked up behind a picture or crucifix at home, or perhaps used as a marker in a missal or prayer book.

On Palm Sunday the passion of Christ is read aloud in church, and we stand throughout, holding our palm branches. Holy Week begins to take on its special atmosphere.

"Jesus' entry into Jerusalem manifested the coming of the kingdom that the King-Messiah was going to accomplish by the Passover of his Death and Resurrection. It is with the celebration of that entry on Palm Sunday that the Church's liturgy solemnly opens Holy Week."[7]

---

[7] *Catechism of the Catholic Church*, 560.

Holy Week

During Holy Week, the statues and crucifixes in the church will be covered with purple cloth. This is a sign that the Church is, in a sense, in mourning. We do not have the usual beauty and brightness that statues bring. Our minds are fixed on the passion and death of Christ.

Maunday Thursday

Spy Wednesday

The old name for the Wednesday of Holy Week is "Spy Wednesday", a reference to the traitor Judas.

The ceremonies of the final days of Holy Week are known as the Easter Triduum because they take place over three days, with the events of Holy Thursday, Good Friday and then Easter.

Thursday is known as Holy Thursday. It is the day when we remember the Last Supper. It is a special day for praying for priests.

"And as they were eating, he took the bread, and blessed, and broke it, and gave it to them and said: 'Take; this is my body.' And he took a cup, and when her had given thanks he gave it to them, and they all drank of it. And he said to them, 'This is my blood of the covenant, which is poured out for many...'" (*Mk* 14:22-23)

Chrism Mass

On Holy Thursday the priests of each diocese come together at the Cathedral for the Chrism Mass. Chrism means "anointing". At the Chrism Mass, the oils which are used for anointing during the coming year are blessed.

They will be used for anointing children - and adults - in baptism and confirmation, and for anointing the sick.

"God our maker,
source of all growth in holiness,
accept the joyful thanks and praise
we offer in the name of your Church.

In the beginning, at your command,
the earth produced fruit-bearing trees.
From the fruit of the olive tree
you have provided us with oil for holy chrism.
The prophet David sang of the life and joy
that the oil would bring us in the sacraments of your love.

After the avenging flood,
the dove returning to Noah with an olive branch
announced your gift of peace.
This was a sign of a greater gift to come.
Now the waters of baptism wash away the sins of men,
and by the anointing with olive oil
you make us radiant with your joy.

At your command,
Aaron was washed with water,
and your servant Moses, his brother,
anointed him priest.
This too foreshadowed greater things to come.
After your Son, Jesus Christ our Lord,

asked John for baptism in the waters of Jordan,
you sent the Spirit upon him
in the form of a dove
and by the witness of your own voice
you declared him to be your only, well-beloved Son.
In this you clearly fulfilled the prophecy of David,
that Christ would be anointed with the oil of gladness
beyond his fellow men.

And so, Father, we ask you to bless
this oil you have created.
Fill it with the power of your Holy Spirit
through Christ your Son.
It is from him that chrism takes its name
and with chrism you have anointed
for yourself priests and kings,
prophets and martyrs...."

(Prayer from the Chrism Mass)

The Chrism Mass is usually held on the morning of Holy Thursday, although in some dioceses it is held earlier in the week. It is open to everyone and is usually very crowded as people come to pray for their priests and to support them. A recent innovation has been giving small cards of appreciation to priests on this day. In some places, people gather outside the Cathedral to show their appreciation to their priests: as the procession, led by the

Bishop approaches, people applaud and even hold up "Thank you" placards.

Maundy

Holy Thursday is also known as Maundy Thursday. Why "Maundy"? It's an old English word, which comes from the Latin, *mandatum*, which also gives us the word "command". What is the command that we are given on Maundy Thursday? It is the great command that Christ gave to his Apostles on the night of the Last Supper: that we must love one another.

To show this love and the spirit of service which is at its heart, Christ washed the feet of his Apostles before supper began. This is still done in Catholic churches around the world. The Pope in Rome ceremonially washes the feet of twelve men, and you can watch this on the internet or on a Catholic television network.

In a longstanding tradition, in past times the Kings and Queens of England washed the feet of twelve poor men on Maundy Thursday, and gave them gifts of money and clothing. Today, this tradition is still honoured in the "Royal Maundy". The Queen attends a special church service, and distributes "Maundy money", specially minted coins that are placed in red and white bags or boxes bearing the royal cipher. Why red and white? These are chosen to represent the blood and water that flowed from the side of Christ on Calvary. The last monarch who actually washed people's feet was James II who ruled from 1685 to 1688.

The Royal Maundy is carried out at a different church or cathedral each year. The Queen is accompanied by Yeoman of the Guard in their traditional costumes, and she is presented with a posy of flowers and herbs. The men and women chosen to receive "Maundy money" usually include people who have done some service in the community and merit this special honour. The number is linked to the Queen's age - thus in 2008 there were 82 men and 82 women. The money, one coin of each denomination, specially minted, is in fact legal currency, (but rarely spent in shops) and usually becomes a cherished family heirloom.

Why not distribute Maundy money in your family? Sort through your change, and find one coin of each denomination. Polish the coins up with metal polish, and put them in a presentation box or envelope with a holy picture, marked with the date. You could add a short explanation about the Maundy tradition. The coins could be given out at suppertime.

Mandatum

In Rome, the Pope also carries out the *Mandatum*, by actually washing the feet of twelve men in a ceremony in St Peter's Basilica. He kneels before each man, and pours water from a great silver ewer on to the man's feet, then wipes them with a linen towel, while a choir sings. It is a moving and impressive ceremony, which has been carried out in just this way for centuries and takes us right back to the night of the Last Supper. It can be seen online.

The *Mandatum* is also carried out in ordinary Catholic parishes. The priest will ceremonially wash the feet of twelve men of the parish, who take their places on the sanctuary for this at the start of Mass. The chants and prayers remind us of Christ's commandment and the importance of love: "*Ubi caritas...*"

Last Supper

The Mass on Holy Thursday is the Mass of the Last Supper. At the start of the *Gloria*, all the bells in the church are rung. They will not be heard again until they ring with the joy of the Resurrection on Easter Sunday. During the solemn hours of Holy Thursday and Good Friday, a wooden clapper is used instead at the points in the Mass when a bell would usually be rung.

There is an old legend that all the bells fly to Rome on the night of Holy Thursday, where they are blessed by the Holy Father. They fly back to the churches in time to be rung joyfully for the first Mass of Easter.

The scripture readings take us back to the night of the Passover, describing the ritual meal that was to be eaten, and the blood of the sacrificed animal that was to be sprinkled on the doorways.

Holy Thursday links us to the Jewish Passover. The Passover feast celebrates how, when the Jewish people were enslaved in Egypt, God brought them their freedom. He gave them a great leader, Moses, who would bring them out of slavery and take them towards the Promised Land. On the night of the Passover, the Jewish people had to eat a special meal.

"This month shall be for you the beginning of months; it shall be the first month of the year for you. Tell all the congregation of Israel that on the tenth day of this month they shall take every man a lamb according to their fathers' houses, a lamb for every household...Your lamb shall be without blemish, a male a year old, you shall take it from the sheep or from the goats; and you shall keep it until the fourteenth day of this month, when the whole assembly of the congregation of Israel shall kill their lambs in the evening. Then they shall take some of the blood, and put it on the two doorposts and the lintel of the houses in which they eat them. They shall eat the flesh that night, roasted; with unleavened bread and bitter herbs they shall eat it..." (*Ex* 12:1-9)

Every year, faithful Jewish people honour the Passover, and remember their covenant with God. We too listen to the scripture reading from the Book of Exodus, and on this holy night at Mass we know that Christ is our Passover Lamb, who offers redemption to all from the slavery of sin.

As the Mass ends, the Blessed Sacrament is taken in procession to an Altar of Repose. This is in a side-chapel, which has been specially decorated with flowers and candles. Here, we can keep watch with Christ, remembering his agony in the garden of Gethsemane. Another tradition is to visit different churches and to pray at the Altar of Repose in each one.

Meanwhile, the main altar of the church is completely stripped - the candles and the altar cloths are taken away, the sanctuary lamp is snuffed out, everything is left bleak and bare. We are reminded of Christ being stripped of his garments when he was nailed to the Cross.

Because of Holy Thursday, every Thursday is a day that commemorates the Last Supper and is dedicated in a special sense to the Eucharist. Many parishes have adoration of the Eucharist all day on Thursdays, with people attending the church for an hour or more, and praying, on that day.

Some families eat a Passover-style supper on Holy Thursday, with roast lamb flavoured with rosemary and accompanied by horseradish (remembering the "bitter herbs" mentioned in the scriptures). You could look up Jewish Passover traditions on the internet and do something with your own family.

Good Friday

"Let us fix our eyes on Christ's blood and understand how precious it is to his Father, for, poured out for our salvation, it has brought to the whole world the grace of repentance." (*St Clement of Rome*)

The old Anglo-Saxon name for Good Friday was "Lang Fredag" or "Long Friday", "long" in the sense of being great and significant. The day is "good" because it is the day that our salvation was won for us by Christ on the Cross, but of course it is a day of sorrow, solemnity, and mourning. The name may also come from the idea of its being "God's Friday".

It is because of Good Friday that every Friday is important for Christians, and observed as a day of penance. As Catholics we are meant to abstain from meat, or to observe some small act of penance, every Friday, throughout the year.

The Liturgy

The central focus of Good Friday is the liturgy solemnly commemorating the passion and death of Christ, usually held in the afternoon at 3pm - the time at which Christ's passion is understood to have taken place. The liturgy begins with the priest and deacon completely prostrating themselves, in silence, in the sanctuary, while the entire congregation also falls to its knees. It is a powerful image of complete and humble submission to God, who took upon himself the weight of our sins and died for us in agony. A cross is brought forward and solemnly unveiled for veneration, which is normally done by kissing it. The Veneration of the Cross is a powerful and moving reminder of what the Cross means to us. The Passion of Christ is then read from the scriptures, and finally Holy Communion is distributed. Mass is not celebrated on Good Friday. Since the Mass of the Last Supper, a great silence has descended on Church around the world.

The Good Friday liturgy has a note of solemnity that is not found on any other day of the year. After Holy Communion and the final blessing, everyone departs in silence. There is no final hymn, and the organ does not play as we leave the church. During the liturgy there have been no bells, only the bleak sound of a wooden clapper. There are no flowers on the altar and the Tabernacle is empty as the Blessed Sacrament has been reserved in a side altar. Everything about Good Friday combines to emphasise that this is the day on which Jesus Christ died on Calvary after hours of suffering.

Traditions

There are many old traditions associated with Good Friday. Because of the action of the soldiers in nailing Christ to the Cross, blacksmiths would not shoe horses on that day, as the work involves hammering nails into the horses' hooves.

The Cross is traditionally said to have been made of wood from the ash tree, which is why that tree always quivers slightly.

Good Friday is said to be a good day for planting seeds - because Christ's blood fell on to the soil and blessed it on that day. Why not buy some flower-seeds and plant them on the afternoon of Good Friday?

Hot Cross buns

The traditional food for Good Friday is the Hot Cross Bun. These are spicy fruit buns, marked with a cross on the top, and eaten hot from the oven. The origin of the hot cross bun is simple: it is eaten on this day of fasting as a replacement for other food. Good Friday is a day when normal meals are not eaten. The Church calls us to fast and to abstain from meat. We can have one main meal, which will be of fish or vegetables.

In some places, hot cross buns are distributed after church, and there are ancient charities which arranged funds for this purpose.

Hot cross buns! Hot cross buns!
One a-penny, two a-penny
Hot cross buns!

Good Friday has for centuries been a day on which normal work is suspended. In recent years, shops have opened and shopping has become a major activity of the day - further evidence of a nationwide retreat from Christian culture.

Good Friday food

Because Good Friday is a fasting day, there should be only one main meal. It is worth planning this well in advance, and establishing a family tradition. Fish pie? Vegetable pie? If you are making anything with pastry, make a pastry cross to place on top before baking.

Witness Walks

A new tradition, which began in the mid-20th century, is that of a "Good Friday Walk of Witness" in which Christians from all the different denominations in a town will join together for a silent procession culminating in a short open-air service of prayers and hymns in a park or shopping centre. Sometimes this includes the erection of a large Cross which will then remain in place all weekend and be decorated with flowers on Easter Sunday morning. A walk of this type usually takes place in the morning.

Easter garden

Good Friday is by tradition a quiet day, not a day for television, shopping, or treats. It is worth planning Good Friday activities well in advance. One activity for the day is the making of an "Easter garden" on a tray - after a walk to gather moss, earth, small pebbles, and some flowers such as daisies and celandines. In one corner there should be a hill, on top of which are three crosses, made of twigs. In another corner white stones make a tomb, with a stone at the door which can be rolled away on Easter morning, when a tiny white piece of cloth can be found inside. You will need some purple cotton or embroidery-silk with which to bind together the small sticks for the three crosses - this could be replaced with golden thread on Easter morning. An Easter garden can also include a little lake, using a mirror or a small dish of water. There can be a pebbled pathway leading up the hill.

In addition to the main afternoon liturgy of Good Friday, most parishes also arrange the Stations of the Cross on Good Friday. Sometimes there is also a special children's liturgy. The Stations of the Cross can also be prayed at home: some families do this by having fourteen lit candles, with one being extinguished as each Station is begun. This slow darkening of the room brings a solemn sense of Good Friday. For the Stations of the Cross you will need fourteen plain white candles. To make them stand upright, slice a potato in half for each candle, scoop out a deep hole for the candle and stick it in. You can make the stands look more attractive by covering the potato-halves in silver foil.

Holy Saturday

On Holy Saturday the Church honours Christ in the tomb. Everything is silent: the Mass is not celebrated, the church is empty. There is an air of expectation. We have celebrated Good Friday, now it is Holy Saturday, and the next day is the third day. And as we recall in the Creed, "On the third day he rose again".

Preparations

Holy Saturday will for most people be a day of preparation for Easter Sunday. There is a lot to do: there will be a special Easter lunch and probably a gathering of friends and family. There will be Easter eggs and perhaps small Easter gifts.

Easter Eggs - Holy Saturday activities

The reason for Easter eggs, as has been explained, is that as a result of the fasting during Lent there were a great many eggs left over by the time Easter arrived. These were decorated and used in lots of different ways.

It is possible to decorate eggs by first blowing out the contents, by making a small hole at the end of each egg and then blowing through the contents into a bowl. The eggs can then be decorated with stickers, or painted. Attaching a small piece of cotton or ribbon with sticky tape will then enable the decorated eggs to be hung on an Easter branch, a centrepiece for the lunch or breakfast table.

(What to do with the contents of the blown eggs? Well, if you aren't fussy, you can just use them for scrambled eggs! Or - an old beauty-hint! - adding a raw egg to shampoo is said to be excellent for bringing a shine to the hair and making it healthy).

It is also possible to dye hard-boiled eggs in their shells. You can buy small pellets of dye mixture along with Easter stickers. Using natural dyes is also possible and it is fun to experiment: boiling up eggs with nettles will produce a shell with a dull green colour; onion skins will produce an orange shade, beetroot a soft pink. Rubbing the eggs afterwards gently with a little olive oil will give them a nice shine.

A Polish tradition is to take a decorated basket of eggs and other Easter breakfast foods to be blessed by the priest during Holy Saturday.

Making small baskets or boxes to hold Easter eggs can be a good Holy Saturday activity too: you can make a small basket for miniature eggs by cutting off the bottom half of an empty washing-up liquid bottle. Metal polish will take off the lettering. Mark off straight lines from the top down to the base, about a quarter of an inch apart, and then cut down these. Weave a narrow ribbon in and out to create a basket, and secure it at the top. Add a ribbon handle, and line the basket with crumpled tissue-paper, ready to be filled with small chocolate eggs on Easter morning.

The Easter Vigil

As the evening of Holy Saturday approaches, the Church prepares to celebrate the Resurrection. People gather at church as darkness falls. The Easter Vigil is one of the most dramatic events of the Church's year. The liturgy of Easter is the summit of the whole of the Church's liturgy. This is the night of all nights, the most glorious of all feasts, the central point on which the whole of our Faith is centred - it is the reason why we celebrate every Sunday in the year and will do until the end of time, it celebrates the most magnificent event of all history, the Resurrection of Jesus Christ from the dead.

The vigil begins with the kindling of the Easter Fire outside the church. Wood has been stacked in a brazier, and this is now lit and burns brightly in the darkness. We gather around it, each person holding a candle. An altar server has brought the great Paschal Candle forward, and as the Vigil begins, grains of incense are inserted into this, with a special prayer - each of the grains representing one of the wounds of Christ.

"May the light of Christ, rising in glory, dispel the darkness of our hearts and minds"[8]

Then the candle is lit from the Easter fire and is carried triumphantly into the church. The priest or deacon sings *Lumen Christi!* and we respond *Deo gratias!* three times,

---

[8] From the prayers of the Easter vigil

each time on a higher note and the joyful sound fills the church, as everyone follows in procession. The light from the Easter candle goes from person to person around the church as we light candles from one another. The darkness is dispelled - Christ is risen, the light has come - it is a wonderfully dramatic moment. Now the deacon stands by the Paschal Candle and sings the *Exultet*, that great joyful hymn of praise which celebrates the glory of the Resurrection as symbolised by this light. The deacon is chosen for this role because he has been ordained to be a "Herald of the Gospel."

"Rejoice, heavenly powers! Sing, choirs of angels!
Exult, all creation around God's throne!
Jesus Christ, our King, is risen!
Sound the trumpet of salvation!

Rejoice, O earth, in shining splendour,
radiant in the brightness of your King!
Christ has conquered! Glory fills you!
Darkness vanishes forever!

Rejoice, O Mother Church! Exult in glory!
The risen Saviour shines upon you!
Let this place resound with joy,
echoing the mighty song of all God's people!"
(*From the Exultet*)

Scripture

The Vigil then continues with scripture readings which take us right from the very beginning, in Genesis, with the creation of all things, through the Book of Exodus with the drama of the Passover and the crossing of the Red Sea, and so to Christ, telling whole story of man's redemption.

The lights are now all on, the altar looks magnificent in its Easter splendour, the vestments are golden and white, and the Mass rings with "alleluias". Christ is risen! At the *Gloria*, all the bells in the church are rung, a glorious sound of joy as the great hymn begins.

Blessing of the baptismal water

The baptismal water is then blessed, and if there are people to be baptised, they are now brought forward to receive baptism with this new water. The Easter Vigil is the traditional time for converts, especially adult converts, to be received into the Church. This has been taking place since the very earliest days of the Church. The new converts have spent Lent in preparation, and now they come forward to make their promises and to receive baptism. We will hear them give their names, and watch as each walks forward and bows his or her head to receive the water of baptism. Each is then given a white garment to wear or to drape around the shoulders. This is always a dramatic moment, as is the renewal of everyone's baptismal promises, the church ringing with the sound of our voices as we once again renounce Satan and all his works, and announce our allegiance to Christ and our full belief in him and in the teachings of the Church. Then the priest sprinkles us all with the fresh new holy water, walking all around the church.

Easter Sunday

Jesus Christ is risen today, Alleluia!
Our triumphant holy day, Alleluia!
Who did once upon the cross, Alleluia!
Suffer to redeem our loss. Alleluia!

Hymns of praise, then, let us sing, Alleluia!
Unto Christ, our praises bring, Alleluia!
Who endured the cross and grave, Alleluia!
Sinners to redeem and save. Alleluia!
(*Easter hymn*)

Although the Easter Vigil is one of the most magnificent events in the Church's year and attendance obviously fulfils the Sunday Mass obligation, there is something special about going to Mass on Easter Sunday morning.

"But on the first day of the week, at early dawn, they went to the tomb, taking the spices which they had prepared. And they found the stone rolled away from the tomb, but when they went in they did not find the body. While they were perplexed about this, behold, two men in white stood by them in dazzling apparel; and as they were frightened and bowed their faces to the ground, the men said to them: 'Why do you seek the living among the dead? He is not here, but has risen'". (*Lk* 24:1-6)

The hymns at Mass will be full of joy and "alleluias". The altar will be surrounded by flowers and candles. The Gospel will tell the glorious story of the Resurrection, the empty tomb, Mary Magdalene and the Apostles.

"Easter is not simply one feast among others, but the "Feast of feasts", the 'Solemnity of solemnities' just as the Eucharist is the 'Sacrament of sacraments'. (*Catechism of the Catholic Church* 1169)

Easter egg hunt

An Easter egg hunt is the traditional activity for Easter morning. There are lots of different ways of doing this: having a large number of very small chocolate eggs - the kind that you buy by the bagful - is best, because they can be hidden in so many unexpected places and take a long time to find. You can put one into the heart of a daffodil, behind a clock, or have two or three in a line on top of a picture. There can also be larger chocolate eggs, and perhaps one or two of the plastic and cardboard sort that have a small gift or sweets inside. Every egg-hunter should have a decorated bag or basket. You can make the hunt fairer by giving each child a specific colour for which to hunt. Sometimes an egg-hunt can be organised with clues like a treasure-hunt.

Hunting for eggs is a very old custom, and obviously related to the simple reality of free-range hens tending to lay their eggs in all sorts of different places. It has a

Christian link in the notion of Mary Magdalene in the garden, looking for Christ, "They have taken away my Lord, and I know not where to find him". Modern commentators tend to say that the eggs are laid by the Easter Bunny, but this is a bit unconvincing since rabbits don't lay eggs. The custom goes back much further than the modern commercialised Easter Bunny image (though that doesn't mean that chocolate bunnies can't be enjoyed at Easter too). No one seems to know how the Easter Bunny originated. Rabbits are associated with fertility - and of course lots of baby bunnies are born at this time of year. An Easter cake decorated with chocolate rabbits can be part of the Easter celebrations, and you can also buy jelly-moulds in rabbit-shapes.

Egg rolling

Another enjoyable Easter tradition is egg-rolling. No one seems to know the origin of this, but many seem to agree that it might be the rolling away of the stone from the mouth of the tomb of the risen Christ. You take your Easter eggs to a park or garden where there is a hillside or slope, and roll them downhill. Only when they hit one another or a stone or other obstacle, and crack open can they be eaten. (Tip: seal the silver-paper wrappers of the eggs with lots of sellotape before you start egg-rolling, otherwise the wrappers come off and you get smashed chocolate over the hillside and nothing to eat!). Some places have egg-rolling races and competitions. If there isn't one in your area, why not start one?

Easter lamb

The traditional dish for Easter Sunday lunch is roast lamb, into which spears of rosemary have been stuck. Rosemary is identified with the "bitter herbs" mentioned in the book of Exodus as part of the Passover meal.

Simnel cake

Simnel cake, associated with Mothering Sunday, is also traditionally eaten on Easter Sunday. A recent popular addition to the tea-table is small "nests" made of chocolate crispy-cakes (made by mixing melted chocolate with cornflakes, forming the mixture into small cakes and then leaving them to set) with two or three small sugar eggs inside. You can also have Easter biscuits, made in the shapes of eggs, Easter lambs, or Easter rabbits.

Eastertide

"Beginning with the Easter Triduum as its source of light, the new age of the Resurrection fills the whole liturgical year with its brilliance..." (*CCC* 1168)

The Easter season lasts for forty days, just as Lent did. Easter only officially ends on the feast of the Ascension, traditionally celebrated on a Thursday, thus making up the exact forty days[9]. All through the Eastertide season you will hear "Alleluia!" in the liturgy at Mass.

In Eastern Europe, there is a tradition of splashing people with water on Easter Monday! As friends and family arrive for a visit, their hosts are waiting in the hall with a dish of water to toss in their faces! While the origin of this remains unclear, it may well be linked with Easter baptism.

Low Sunday

The first Sunday after Easter is sometimes called "Low Sunday". This is an ancient title and the origin is not known - perhaps it is simply "low" after the "high" of Easter.

In 2000, with effect from 2001, it was officially designated as Divine Mercy Sunday. This is a new devotion that began with visions to a Polish nun, Sister Faustina, in a

---

[9] At present in England and Wales it has been moved to the nearest Sunday, by a decision of the Bishops' Conference.

convent at Krakow in the 1930s. She saw an image of Christ with two streams of light pouring from his heart, one white and one red. He revealed to her that this represented his Mercy, which he wanted to pour out to the world. Pope John Paul II, as Archbishop of Krakow, took a particular interest in the Divine Mercy, and as Pope he extended the feast of the Divine Mercy to the whole world. It is very fitting that it is celebrated immediately after Easter. It is rather touching to note, incidentally, that Pope John Paul II died during the vigil of Divine Mercy Sunday.

On the Sundays of Eastertide, the readings at Mass tell us about Christ's appearances to his disciples following his resurrection. The miracle of his resurrection is at the heart of our faith, and we can say with St Thomas: "My Lord and my God".

Ascensiontide

The nine days between Christ's Ascension into heaven, and the coming of the Holy Spirit at Pentecost were spent by the Apostles in prayer. This was the original "novena" - a name we still give to the tradition of praying for nine consecutive days when there is something special that we want to ask of God.

At the Ascension, Christ went back to his Father in heaven.

"So then the Lord Jesus, after he has spoken to them, was taken up into heaven, and sat down at the right hand of God." (*Mk* 16:19)

The days before the feast of the Ascension are the "Rogation days" from the Latin *rogare*, meaning "to ask". Rogation processions are still sometimes held, around the fields asking for a blessing on the land and on the newly-planted crops. Some churches near the sea have a blessing of the water and the fishing-boats, for the harvest of the sea.

Processions

The Rogation processions of long ago gave their names to various places, such as "Gospel Oak", where the Gospel would be read, or "Paternoster field" where the "Our Father" would be said.

A linked tradition is that of "beating the bounds", with processions around the parish boundaries. This seems to have been started after the Reformation, when the old rogation processions were formally banned, but people missed them and so they were turned into walks around the parish borders with stern reminders about knowing where the boundaries were. Might it be possible to arrange for a Rogation procession in your parish, perhaps blessing a parish garden? And what about a walk around the parish boundaries - perhaps with stops for prayers, a decade of the Rosary, or a blessing of a particular spot? This could be a project for young people in the parish - to discover the boundaries of the parish and map out a route.

An old English rural tradition at Ascensiontide is decorating and blessing wells, and thanking God for the gift of pure water. Some villages have beautiful floral "well dressings" depicting Biblical scenes and local saints. Is there some local well or fountain - perhaps one that has become overgrown, vandalised, or forgotten, that could be cleaned up as a parish venture, and then blessed and decorated at Ascensiontide?

Pentecost

Fifty days after Easter comes the great feast of Pentecost - from the Greek word "Pente" meaning "Fifty".

Christ promised that we would not be left alone when he returned to Heaven at the Ascension. At Pentecost the Holy Spirit descended on the Church.

The feast goes back to the days of the Old Testament, when the Jewish people celebrated the Covenant with God at this time. Because of this celebration, people had gathered in Jerusalem from great distances. The Apostles, together with Mary, were gathered together in an Upper Room.

"And suddenly a sound came from heaven like the rush of a mighty wind, and it filled all the house where they were sitting. And there appeared to them tongues, as of fire, distributed and resting on each one of them. And they were all filled with the Holy Spirit and began to speak in other tongues, as the Spirit gave them utterance". (Ac 2:2-5)

Pentecost can be celebrated with paper cut-outs of tongues of fire, perhaps with each one listing one of the

Gifts of the Holy Spirit: wisdom, understanding, counsel, fortitude, knowledge, piety, fear of the Lord.

Fruits of the Holy Spirit

You could also mark the twelve Fruits of the Holy Spirit by having a fruit salad with twelve different sorts of fruit in it: use dried fruits (currants, raisins, dates) and tinned fruits (mandarin oranges, grapefruit) as well as fresh fruits, and combine them with a syrup made with sugar and water and perhaps a dash of your favourite liqueur.

The twelve Fruits of the Holy Spirit are: Charity, Generosity, Joy, Gentleness, Peace, Faithfulness, Patience, Modesty, Kindness, Self-control, Goodness, and Chastity.

Whitsunday

The old name for Pentecost is "Whitsunday", commemorating the white robes worn by the newly-baptised on this day. You could mark this by having everyone wear something white - a shirt, or a white scarf, or a white hanky in a top pocket - and serving some white food such as meringues or a sponge-cake topped with white icing.

A new chapter began at Pentecost, and the Apostles started to take the Gospel of salvation to the whole world. That is our task too. The message of Easter and of the Church is not something we keep to ourselves: it is the glorious news that we must take to everyone: the love of God, the forgiveness of sins, and the redemption of the human race.